HOME
COOKING
with JAPAN'S FIRST LADY

HOME COOKING
with JAPAN'S FIRST LADY
Family Dishes from the Hatoyama Kitchen

MIYUKI HATOYAMA

photographs by **Hironori Handa**

KODANSHA INTERNATIONAL
Tokyo • New York • London

Distributed in the United States by Kodansha America LLC, and in the United Kingdom and continental Europe by Kodansha Europe Ltd.

Published by Kodansha International Ltd., 17–14 Otowa 1-chome, Bunkyo-ku, Tokyo 112–8652.

First edition, 2010
20 19 18 17 16 15 14 13 12 11 10   10 9 8 7 6 5 4 3 2 1

Library of Congress Cataloging-in-Publication Data

Hatoyama, Miyuki.
  [Yokoso Hatoyama resutoran e. English]
  Home cooking with Japan's first lady : family dishes from the Hatoyama kitchen / Miyuki Hatoyama ; photographs by Hironori Handa. -- 1st ed.
     p. cm.
  Includes index.
  ISBN 978-4-7700-3131-0
  1. Cookery, Japanese. I. Title.
  TX724.5.J3H3845 2010
  641.5952--dc22
                    2009052190

www.kodansha-intl.com

C O N T E N T S

MY BEST RECIPES

OUR COMFORT FOOD

FOREWORD

My wife Miyuki announced she had started making pottery before I was even aware she was interested in it. She also made a gorgeous stained-glass window and Tiffany-style lamp shades. She is tremendously creative, always occupying herself with arts and crafts, from painting to pottery and, of course, cooking. Miyuki has never learned any techniques from books and is a wonderful person who expresses herself without artifice.

To cook, first you need to visualize the desired result. Next, you have to decide on the flavor, and then the food has to be arranged nicely on the dish. You need your own touch to add interest to the dish. I am often moved by how creative my wife's cooking is, and the beauty of her arrangements. Her food makes me see cooking as an art.

Miyuki believes that cooking is one way to express her affection for family and friends, so it is no wonder that my son and I have been very happy at our dinner table for many years. She often opens her "Hatoyama Restaurant" for us at midnight when we come home late. I remember so many things we have eaten around midnight… *Jjiage* Korean Hotpot with Seafood, *Nikujaga* Beef and Potatoes, Rice Bowl with Soy-marinated Tuna. Sometimes we have just eaten hamburgers or ready-made meals bought from specialty stores. But what has always been important for us is to eat the same food, at the dining table, together, with conversation. Eating together around the table is one way we catch up with each other and affirm our mutual love. Now my son has set out on his own, and we are very busy with government work. However, we always find time to sit down together and chat over dishes she has lovingly prepared. This cookbook reminds me of many happy memories, and that happiness will always remain in my heart.

Yukio Hatoyama

鳩山由紀夫

INTRODUCTION

My first, happy experience entertaining people with my own food was with my husband Yukio, at that time a graduate student at Stanford University, California. I was in my late twenties, and had just begun discovering the joy of cooking for someone else. When his friends came over for dinner, I wanted to cook Japanese food that they might like, such as barbecued *unagi* eel, or fried chicken marinated in soy sauce. Whenever they gave me a kind of compliment, I was so thrilled that I was motivated to entertain them more often. I was so inspired on one occasion when serving sushi that I went out of my way to build a small sushi counter displaying the various kinds of fish! Our friends and acquaintances started affectionately calling our place "Hatoyama Restaurant."

Ironically, it was only after I went to America that I really started cooking Japanese food. My father was born and grew up in the U.S., and worked as a trade merchant going back and forth between Japan and the States. There was always bacon, ham, and butter in the refrigerator at home, and my mother cooked Western food every day. My favorite foods by the time I was twenty were steak and bread. I only came to learn the beauty of Japanese cooking after living in San Francisco and visiting Japanese restaurants there. I thought professional chefs did an amazing job, preparing food efficiently with no wasted motion. I was fascinated by how they worked in the kitchen, and gradually became interested in cooking myself. At first, I occupied myself with simple things such as cutting store-bought fish fillets sashimi-style and arranging them on a plate. Gradually I took on more sophisticated tasks such as making *dashi* stock from scratch, and scaling and gutting whole fish. From a social perspective, the American parties I was invited to in the '60s influenced me a lot. Yukio and I loved the casual atmosphere with which our hosts always welcomed people, where food and conversation were equally important. This book contains a lot of recipes that I learned in those days, by talking to friends and scribbling down recipes on scraps of paper.

Before Yukio went to the U.S. to study, he lived with his parents and grandmother in Tokyo, in a classic British-style house, built in 1924, with a large dining room and nice porcelain. Dignitaries, secretaries, and journalists

socialized constantly and his mother always said the front hallway was like a public street! His grandfather was a three-term prime minister, and many people visited the house to pay their respects and seek favors. His mother was always busy running the house and supporting her husband, so meals were customary and simple, bordering on lean and humble. The dish he remembers most from his mother's cooking is grilled salt-dried salmon. It's a typical Japanese dinner, good with a bowl of white rice. Grilled salmon has become his soul food, and so for me also it's an emotionally meaningful dish that reminds me of him.

My recipes are products of my experience; more than simply instructions for preparing food, they are infused with the time, place, occasion, and people who helped create the memories. We find more easily, or adore more deeply, the beauty of our own traditions by knowing and understanding those of others. For Yukio and me, the experience of living in the U.S. and feeling the patriotic spirit in America made us realize our love for our own country. As we travel to other countries together, we are always fascinated with the culture and food, and at the same time, appreciate the virtues of our own. By bringing that spirit to our table and our lives, our dinner time is always happy. I hope your table is also brightened by beautiful experiences and memories, full of love and the joy of cooking. Achieving this is easier than you may think if you open up your mind to the world.

Miyuki Hatoyama

FAMILY FAVORITES

My family prefers to come home for dinner after work, rather than dining out. These are their favorite recipes. I don't usually measure ingredients, but I experimented for this book and wrote down the right amounts. Enjoy!

Chicken Wings with Soy Sauce and Seasoning Salt

I started using seasoning salt when I lived in San Francisco. It is such a versatile ingredient that I even use it for many of my Japanese dishes. The key to this recipe is to cut open each chicken wing into a flat piece and fry it until the skin is extra crispy. My son has moved out now, but when he was a teenager he ate these by the dozen!

MAKES 16 PIECES

16 chicken wings (use only the middle part with two thin bones, not the base or the tip)

Marinade
2 ½ Tbsp soy sauce
2 ½ Tbsp *mirin*
1 large knob ginger

Seasoning salt to taste
About ½ cup potato starch (or cornstarch), for dusting
Oil for deep-frying
1 *naganegi* onion or other sweet onion, shredded
1 lemon, cut into 8 wedges

1 Peel the knob of ginger and grate. Squeeze the juice from the gratings and put in a bowl. Add the soy sauce and *mirin*. Set aside.

2 A chicken wing has two bones: a thin bone and a thick bone. First, cut into the underside of the wing down to the thin bone, then make another, parallel cut down to the thicker bone. Spread open the meat as much as possible to make a larger, flatter piece. Add the chicken pieces to the marinade and leave for 30 minutes.

3 Preheat the oil for deep-frying to 340°F (170°C).

4 Put the potato starch in a shallow tray or bowl. Blot dry the chicken wings with paper towels, rub with the seasoning salt, and lightly coat with the potato starch.

5 Deep-fry the chicken wings until browned and crispy. Serve on a bed of shredded onion and garnish with lemon wedges.

Baked Crepes with Chicken and Béchamel

My husband and son often crave something creamy and rich, like pasta gratin or chicken fricassee. These baked crepes always do the trick. You can prepare them in the baking dish in advance, and bake them just before you sit down to eat.

MAKES 8 TO 10 CREPES

Crepes
- 1 cup flour
- A pinch of salt
- 2 eggs
- 1 cup whole milk
- 2 ½ Tbsp unsalted butter, melted
- Extra butter for greasing the pan

Béchamel
- 3 Tbsp unsalted butter
- 4 Tbsp flour
- 2 cups whole milk
- Salt and black pepper to taste

10 ½ oz. (300 g) chicken thighs, without skin
1 yellow onion
1 Tbsp vegetable oil
Melted butter for brushing on crepes
Parmesan cheese for topping

These crepes are even better when the edges and the cheese on top are browned a little bit and release an appetizing aroma throughout the kitchen. They're easy to serve, and taste great even when cold.

1 Start by making the crepes. Mix the flour, salt, and eggs in a bowl with a whisk until well combined. Heat the milk to 140°F (60°C) and whisk into the bowl little by little. Stir in the melted butter, cover with a damp cloth, and leave for 30 minutes.

2 Heat a frying pan and lightly grease with the extra butter. Add a ladleful of crepe batter and swirl the pan so that the batter covers the bottom of the pan evenly. Cook until the surface looks dry, then flip the crepe over and briefly cook the other side. Remove the crepe to a plate, reheat the pan, repeat for the rest of the batter.

3 To make the béchamel, heat the butter in a saucepan over low heat until melted. Add the flour and cook, stirring constantly with a spatula to prevent browning. Stir in the milk little by little, then raise the heat to medium-low and bring to a simmer. Once the béchamel simmers and thickens, remove from the heat and season with salt and pepper. Dice the chicken thighs and onion into ½-in. (1-cm) cubes and sauté in vegetable oil until fully cooked. Stir in the béchamel.

4 Spoon the chicken and béchamel mixture on the front half of each crepe and roll the crepes around the mixture. Arrange the rolled crepes in a baking dish, brush with melted butter and top with Parmesan cheese. Bake at 390 to 425°F (200 to 220°C) in an oven for 6 to 8 minutes until the tops are browned.

Daikon Radish and Beef Slices

We Japanese love daikon radish simmered for a long time until meltingly tender, but I wanted to find a way of cooking daikon quicker for home meals. I cut the daikon into very thin rounds and simmer them along with thinly sliced beef. It cooks in ten minutes and is so good!

SERVES FOUR

¼ daikon radish

3 ½ oz. (100 g) paper-thin slices of beef
  from chuck, rib or loin

1 Tbsp sugar

½ Tbsp sake

½ Tbsp *mirin*

1½ Tbsp soy sauce

½ cup water

1 large knob ginger, cut into slivers

1 Peel the daikon radish and cut into very thin rounds.

2 Spread a quarter of the daikon rounds on the bottom of a large saucepan, then spread a quarter of the beef slices. Repeat three times. Combine the sugar, sake, *mirin*, soy sauce, and water in a bowl and add to the pan. Bring the pan to a gentle simmer over medium heat, cover with a lid and cook, skimming off the foam from time to time, until the daikon rounds are tender. Sprinkle with the ginger slivers and serve.

I always cook thinking, "How can I cook quickly so my family doesn't have to wait when they come home late and hungry?"

Stir-fried Squid and Kimchi

I rarely cook complicated dishes in my home, or anything that requires a lot of labor-intensive preparation. I'm just not into that. There is a great Korean food market in our neighborhood in Tokyo, and the kimchi there is fantastic, so I often use it in my cooking. I experimented with this dish by adding walnuts, giving it a lively crunch and a pleasant nutty flavor.

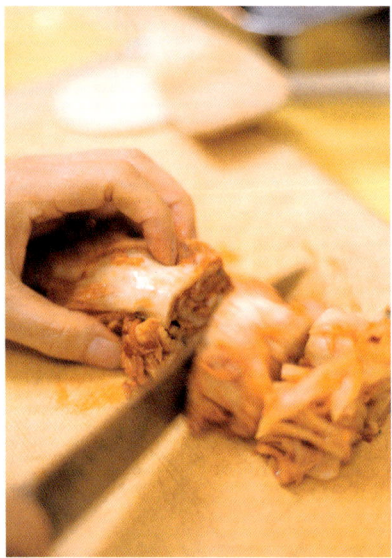

SERVES FOUR

7 oz. (200 g) squid or calamari, thawed if frozen

10 ½ oz. (300 g) kimchi of Napa cabbage

½ bunch *shungiku* greens (or baby spinach)

⅓ cup walnut halves, roughly chopped

1 small dried red chili pepper (optional)

2 Tbsp roasted sesame oil

1 Blot dry the squid mantle or calamari well. If using the mantle (the head section), score in a crosshatch pattern at about ⅛-in. (3-mm) intervals and cut into pieces. The tentacles can be used as-is. Cut the kimchi into pieces. Pick the leaves off *shungiku* greens (use only the leaves, not the tough stem). Lightly toast the walnuts. If using a dried red chili pepper, soak in water to soften, cut in half lengthwise, remove the seeds and cut into slivers.

2 Heat a large frying pan or a wok, and add the roasted sesame oil. Add the squid or calamari and walnuts and stir-fry over high heat. Add the kimchi and chili pepper and continue to stir-fry until the squid or calamari is cooked and the kimchi is heated through. Add the shungiku greens, swirl the pan briefly, and serve.

Yellowtail Shabu-shabu

My husband and I love yellowtail shabu-shabu (hotpot) even more than beef shabu-shabu. It is so much fun to eat together from the same pot, sharing hot food during the cold winter. If you have a portable gas burner or a tabletop charcoal grill, arrange the ingredients on a large platter and cook them all right at the table.

SERVES FOUR

10 ½ oz. (300 g) *buri* yellowtail fillet, sashimi quality
1 block soft tofu, about 12 oz. (340 g)
1 bunch *mitsuba* herb or watercress
6 cups water
¼ cup sake
1 Tbsp soy sauce
bottled *ponzu* sauce

Suggestion for condiments

Freshly ground black pepper
Chili flakes
Grated daikon radish
Chopped scallions

1 Cut the yellowtail into thin slices. Cut the tofu into 8 pieces. Cut the *mitsuba* herb or watercress into 2-in. (5-cm) lengths.

2 In a medium to large, shallow pan, bring the water and sake to a boil. Add the soy sauce. Add the yellowtail, tofu, and mitsuba herb or watercress and quickly bring the pot to the table. The ingredients will be barely cooked, just heated through. Immediately eat by dipping in individual dishes of *ponzu* sauce, along with any combination of condiments.

Jjigae Korean Hotpot with Seafood

Jjigae is a fantastic Korean hotpot with a lot of healthy seafood, and yes, a lot of red chili pepper. The flavors from the kimchi and *gochujang* (fermented chili paste) make the dish surprisingly satisfying. My love for Korean food began when I visited the country with my husband almost fifteen years ago. Since then, I've tried to recreate many Korean dishes at my house, and my husband often asks me to make them.

SERVES FOUR

7oz. (200 g) fresh *kalguksu* Korean wheat noodles, or 3 ½ oz. (100 g) dried udon noodles, per serving

½ block soft tofu, about 6 oz. (170 g)

1 *naganegi* onion or other sweet onion

1 bunch *shungiku* greens or spinach

10 oz. (280 g) kimchi

2 precooked king crab legs in the shell, thawed if frozen

1 medium squid mantle (or calamari), thawed if frozen

7 oz. (200 g) cod fillet

Stock

| 2 bouillon cubes, preferably beef
| 4 cups water
| 3 Tbsp *gochujang* fermented chili paste
| 2 Tbsp yellow miso
| 2 Tbsp soy sauce

1   Cook the noodles in boiling water until soft but still crunchy, drain using a sieve and set aside.

2   Cut the tofu into chunks. Cut the onion into chunks. Pick the leaves off the *shungiku* greens.

3   Lightly squeeze out the kimchi and chop into 1-in. (2- to 3-cm) lengths. Cut lengthwise into the shell of each crab leg to make it easier to eat. Cut the squid and cod into bite-size pieces.

4   Put all ingredients of the stock in a large pot over high heat and add the squid and cod. Bring to a boil, skim the surface, and lower the heat to medium. Add the kimchi and noodles, and continue to simmer for 5 minutes until the seafood is cooked through. Add the crab, onion, and shungiku greens and continue to simmer for 3 minutes until the crab is heated through. Divide the noodles into individual serving bowls, then add the seafood, vegetables and broth. Eat while hot.

Deep-fried Octopus with Leaf Lettuce

My husband loves octopus in salad for its chewy texture and rich flavor, contrasting with the fresh, crisp salad greens. I often make this dish thinking of his smile. Other vegetables can be substituted for the green leaf lettuce, such as fresh Napa cabbage or spinach. This dish works well with deep-fried calamari, shrimp, or scallops, but in my house it is always octopus.

SERVES FOUR

1 Tbsp soy sauce

1 Tbsp sake

½ Tbsp *mirin*

1 or 2 pieces precooked octopus (about 7 oz./200 g in total), thawed if frozen

2 *naganegi* onions, white part only (or 1 sweet onion, such as red, Vidalia or Maui)

1 small cucumber (or ⅓ English cucumber, peeled)

⅓ head green leaf lettuce

Dressing

½ cup Hatoyama Dressing (page 98)

1 tsp Dijon mustard

1 tsp balsamic vinegar (optional)

Salt and black pepper to taste

½ cup flour

Oil for deep-frying

1 Combine the soy sauce, sake, and *mirin* in a medium bowl. Slice the octopus as thinly as possible, add to the bowl and allow to marinate for 10 to 15 minutes.

2 Cut the onions into thin slices. Place the cucumber on the cutting board and lightly sprinkle with salt. Roll the cucumber in the salt to soften the skin, rinse with water, and pat dry. Cut the cucumber into thin rounds. Tear the lettuce into chunks by hand.

3 Preheat the oil for deep-frying to 340°F (170°C). Combine all ingredients of the dressing and set aside.

4 Put the flour in a small bowl. Lay the octopus slices on a paper towel and blot dry. Dust the octopus slices with the flour and deep-fry in the oil until heated through.

5 In a large bowl, combine the onion, cucumber, lettuce, and octopus. Add the dressing, toss and serve.

Pickled Napa Cabbage

Most people I know are surprised to hear I make home-made pickled cabbage. When I was living in Califor-nia, I dearly wanted to eat Japanese-style pickles, so I needed to find a way to make them by myself. I found Napa cabbage grown by a local farmer, bought a fairly large enameled steel container, and started pickling. I enjoyed the results, and gave away the pickles to my friends. Among the countless variations of pickled cabbage in Japan, my favorite is pre-pared with grated onion, ginger, and plenty of dried red chili peppers. I don't break open the dried peppers, so they add only a mild spice to the pickles. After I came back to Japan, I once made this in a sake barrel for my son's kindergarten party, and it was very popular among the mothers there. The event still evokes good memories for me and my son, and because the pickles taste better when pickled in a larger batch, I wrote this recipe for pickling in a barrel. However, pickling should be fun and easy, and can be done using a reg-ular kitchen bowl or food-safe plastic container. I've added the method for making a small batch in the note.

Equipment

- A 9 ½ gallon (36 L) clean container, about 18 in. (45 cm) in diameter and 18 in. (45 cm) high
- Two 18-lb. (8-kg) weights
- Grater
- Large plastic bag

4 large heads Napa cabbage, 18 lbs. (8 kg) in total

2 large knobs ginger

1 large onion

A large handful dried red chili peppers, medium-hot, about ⅔ cup

8 in. (20 cm) dried *kombu* kelp

1 ¼ cups (8 ½ oz./240 g) sea salt

TO EAT AND SERVE

You can begin eating the cabbage two days after pickling starts. Check the taste each day. The pickles will start out salty, then become pleasantly sour from lactic acid fermentation. When the taste is to your liking, it is a good idea to transfer the pickles into a smaller, clean container and refrigerate. I enjoy my pickles for 2 months this way. To serve, rinse the cabbage leaves in water, cut into bite-sized pieces, and arrange on a plate. Top with finely sliced *kombu* and red chili peppers, if desired. If the pickles becomes too sour, either in the barrel or in the refrigerator, do not eat but discard.

1 Cut each cabbage into eight wedges, wash and let stand to drain well. Peel the ginger and onion. Cut the dried *kombu* kelp into strips using scissors.

2 Lightly sprinkle about 2 Tbsp salt on the bottom of the container. Divide the remaining salt into five roughly equal parts.

3 Tightly pack wedges of cabbage in the barrel, cut-side up. Generously sprinkle with a portion of salt, ¼ of the dried kombu kelp, and ¼ of the dried red chili. Grate ¼ of the onion and ¼ of the ginger onto the cabbage wedges, covering them evenly.

4 Repeat three times to have four layers of cabbage. Stack each layer of cabbage wedges so it is not directly aligned with the layer below. In this way, the wedges will overlap. Finish by evenly sprinkling the last portion of salt over the top.

5 Cover the container with a large plastic bag, put a flat, round disk (see note for details) directly on the cabbage, and press down. Place the two weights on top and leave in a cool place.

6 The cabbages begin releasing water in about two days, and are pickled in the resulting brine. When the liquid rises above the cabbages (usually after three or four days), remove one of the weights. Continue pickling.

Note In Step 5, a flat disk is used for evenly pressing down the Napa cabbage. Use a flat disk of wood, a small, round tray, or a dish a little smaller than the diameter of the container.

When using a medium-sized bowl or plastic container instead of a barrel, use ¼ to ½ head Napa cabbage. Separate the leaves or cut them into large pieces. Use 3% to 5% salt by weight of the Napa cabbage (about 1 to 1½ tablespoons of salt), a few dried red chili peppers, and a stamp-sized piece of *kombu* kelp. You can omit the grated ginger and onion. Make fewer layers of cabbage—two or three—sprinkling salt on each layer. Find a disk or plate that fits inside the bowl or container and weigh the disk down with a rock or paperweight. Leave in a cool place or refrigerate. The pickling time will be much shorter, from one day to three days.

PRIDE IN COOKING

I often hear my husband saying to me, "Why don't you take a break? Relax a little, maybe read a book." If it isn't cleaning, washing, or some other household chore, I'm usually cooking or preparing and pickling vegetables. I'm just not the type of person who can kick back and relax; I always need to be doing something. My body seems to move as my brain thinks. I picture what to do in my mind as a game plan, which I think helps make my recipes very simple, quick, and easy to prepare. I have always been a housewife who loves cooking for my family, and I simply wouldn't be able to do this without having an efficient way of working. I don't want to be too extravagant with my food, and I don't want to waste time. My policy is that great taste is made not so much by spending a great deal of time, but more through work, care, and affection—in other words, with love.

My mother was actually not very much into cooking. She preferred to immerse herself in dense books in the living room rather than spend her time making food in the kitchen. She also had to work very hard, raising me as a single mother after my father died when I was ten. Like all Japanese children, I took to school a *bento* lunch box made by my mother, but mine was always just a simple sandwich with raw vegetables. I remember that I yearned for a nicer bento lunch like my friends had, with rice, fish, meat, and side dishes. I even tried making it myself, imitating my friends' lunches by sautéing ground beef and putting it on rice, without realizing you have to season the beef!

Still, my mother knew some great recipes that I make even now and my son loves, too. She was very good at making fried rice with only garlic, beef, eggs, and seasoning salt. My husband's mother influences my cooking, too. In Japan, Russian-style stuffed cabbage rolls are very popular, but hers are the best I've had anywhere, and I recall that my husband's grandfather, as prime minister, was instrumental in restoring diplomatic ties between Japan and Russia.

My cooking memories—bitter or sweet—remain lively and colorful. They motivate me to always endeavor to cook better. I love to create new memories with my husband and with my son, who lives on his own now but often visits, looking forward (I hope!) to my cooking. With their love and support, I'm proud of my food.

FAST APPETIZERS

I don't want to make my hungry family wait at the table, or make guests sit uncomfortably while I am stuck in the kitchen. I like to have these home-style appetizers ready to be served at the drop of a hat.

Prosciutto and Cream Cheese Salad

Many people make a salad using prosciutto, but wanting to add a twist, I tried wrapping a stick of cream cheese in the prosciutto. My guests are always surprised at the hidden taste—it just goes to show what a simple trick can do—and I get a lot of compliments. Prepare everything in advance and refrigerate the salad and dressing separately. All you need to do when your guests sit down at the table is toss the salad with the dressing.

SERVES FOUR

About 5 oz. (140 g) cream cheese, kept cool

16 slices prosciutto, kept cool

16 chives

A 4-in. (10-cm) cylindrical piece of daikon radish

¼ head leaf lettuce

¼ head curly endive

4 to 5 radishes

½ pack (about 3 ½ oz./100 g) cremini mushrooms (or *shimeji* mushrooms)

1 Tbsp olive oil

½ cup chopped scallions

4 slices lemon

½ cup Hatoyama Dressing (page 98)

1 Divide the cream cheese into 16 pieces, roll each piece in a slice of prosciutto, and tie with a chives leaf.

2 Peel the daikon and cut into paper-thin rounds. Rinse the leaf lettuce and curly endive in cold water and tear into bite-size pieces. Trim the radishes and cut lengthwise into thin rounds.

3 Trim and cut the cremini mushrooms into pieces. Heat the olive oil in a small frying pan and sauté the mushrooms.

4 In a large bowl, combine the prosciutto rolls, daikon, lettuce, curly endive, radish, cremini, chopped scallions, and lemon slices. Add the dressing, toss and serve.

Carpaccio-style Tuna with Creamy Dressing

Carpaccio is actually a beef dish, so I've called this recipe "carpaccio-style" tuna. The creamy dressing has a mayonnaise base with a hint of soy sauce, and accompanies raw tuna slices very well. It also goes well with raw beef slices, roast beef, seared scallops, and shrimp.

SERVES FOUR

10 ½ oz. (300 g) sashimi-grade fillet of fresh tuna
2 sprigs Italian parsley, leaves plucked
2 sprigs oregano, leaves only
½ tsp pink peppercorns
2 lemon slices

Creamy Dressing

1 Tbsp capers (bottled in vinegar)
2 tsp mayonnaise
2 tsp lemon juice
2 ½ Tbsp rice vinegar
3 Tbsp olive oil
½ tsp soy sauce
1 tsp grated onion
A pinch of salt

I enjoy the combination of carpaccio-style tuna and a light-bodied red wine.

1 Cut the tuna into ⅛-in. (3-mm) thick bite-size slices and arrange on a serving dish. If the room is hot, cover and keep in the refrigerator.

2 For the creamy dressing: Finely chop the capers and put in a medium bowl, add the other dressing ingredients, and whip to a creamy consistency. Adjust to taste with soy sauce or salt.

3 Spoon the dressing over the tuna slices. Sprinkle with the Italian parsley, oregano, and pink peppercorns, arranging the lemon slices on the side.

Salmon Terrine Salad

When my husband Yukio and I lived in San Francisco, we were often invited to parties. We loved how Americans threw informal parties and served casual dishes, and I encountered many easy but beautiful recipes that I am always making back here in Japan. This is one of those dishes—using chunks of fluffy terrine made from canned salmon! I have such fond memories of warm, friendly conversations at parties, standing for hours, eating salmon terrine and sipping glasses of wine.

SERVES FOUR

7 oz. (200 g) easy salmon terrine (see recipe
   on the right)

About 7 oz. (200 g) salad greens, single-kind or
   mixed, such as romaine, green leaf lettuce,
   baby spinach, or Bibb lettuce

½ red bell pepper

½ yellow bell pepper

½ onion

2 Tbsp tomato ketchup

2 Tbsp mayonnaise

1 Tbsp lemon juice

1 Tear the salad greens by hand into bite-size pieces. Remove the seeds from the bell peppers and cut into small cubes. Cut the onion into thin slices, allow to soak in ice water for 20 minutes to remove harshness, drain, and blot dry. Cut the salmon terrine into bite-size pieces. Put these ingredients into a large bowl.

2 Combine the tomato ketchup, mayonnaise, and lemon juice in a small bowl and add to the large bowl. Gently toss and serve.

Easy Salmon Terrine

I use canned salmon: not the oil-packed kind, but the kind which is packed in brine.

**MAKES ONE 3½ × 7-IN.
(9 × 18-CM) RECTANGLE**

7 to 8 oz. (about 220 g) canned salmon

1 Tbsp powdered gelatin, about ⅓ oz.
   (10 g)

1 Tbsp chopped onion

1 Tbsp chopped celery

1 Tbsp white wine

1 tsp lemon juice

½ cup heavy cream

1 cup mayonnaise

Lemon wedges to serve

Sprigs of Italian parsley to serve

1 Combine the powdered gelatin and 4 Tbsp water in a small, microwave-safe container and heat in a microwave for 30 seconds. Stir to dissolve completely.

2 Drain the canned salmon and remove any bones. In a food processor, combine the salmon, onion, celery, dissolved gelatin, wine, lemon juice, heavy cream, and mayonnaise and mix for about 3 minutes, until pureed smoothly. Pour the mixture into the mold and refrigerate until set.

3 To remove from the mold, dip the mold in tepid water for a few seconds, cover with a flat dish and flip. Cut the terrine into pieces and serve with the lemon wedges and sprigs of Italian parsley.

Asparagus and Avocado with Consommé Jelly

I use store-bought consommé for this recipe, set with gelatin and broken into pieces, which adds an upscale feeling to an otherwise ordinary salad. Keep some consommé jelly in the refrigerator—it really makes a difference to this recipe that your family and guests will notice. Before gelling the consommé, you can add chopped capers or any fragrant herb.

SERVES FOUR

1¼ cup consommé soup or other broth, store-bought

4 tsp (10 g) powdered gelatin, soaked in 4 Tbsp water prior to use

2 tsp salt

10 medium to large spears green asparagus

½ ripe avocado

20 cherry tomatoes

2 tsp chopped scallions or chives

1 Pour the consommé soup in a small saucepan and warm. Add the soaked gelatin and dissolve completely. Pour into a shallow container and refrigerate until set (3 to 4 hours).

2 Bring plenty of water to a boil in a large pot and add 2 tsp salt. Trim each asparagus spear, blanch, drain, and cut into bite-size lengths. Cut the avocado into halves by inserting a knife around the length, and remove the seed in the center. Peel and cut into chunks. Halve the cherry tomatoes.

3 Combine the asparagus, avocado, and tomatoes in a large bowl and add the consommé jelly, breaking it up with a spoon. Lightly toss, arrange on individual serving dishes, and sprinkle each with chopped scallions or chives.

Baked Napa Cabbage *en Cocotte*

Most food at my parties is laid out in individual servings, on plates and in bowls, since I'm worried about guests hesitating to serve themselves. Serving food in individual dishes, as in this recipe *en cocotte*, says to guests "please, you should eat this much at least!" I use canned salmon packed in brine here as well as in the Easy Salmon Terrine recipe (page 36).

MAKES FOUR 8-IN. (20-CM) *COCOTTES*

¼ Napa cabbage, about 14 oz. (400 g)

2 tsp salt

8 oz. (about 220 g) canned salmon

4 to 5 oz. (120 to 150 g) mozzarella cheese, cut into slices or small cubes

4 tsp *panko* bread crumbs

Béchamel

2 bouillon cubes

2 cups whole milk

4 Tbsp butter

5 Tbsp flour

Salt and black pepper to taste

1 Bring plenty of water to a boil in a large pot and add 2 tsp salt. Trim the end of the Napa cabbage, separate the leaves, blanch them and drain. Save 1 cup of the blanching water. Cut the cabbage into chunks.

2 Making béchamel: Dissolve the bouillon cubes in the 1 cup of blanching water saved in step 1. Mix with the milk. Heat the butter in a saucepan over low heat until melted. Add the flour and cook, stirring constantly with a spatula to prevent browning. Stir in the milk and bouillon mixture little by little, then raise the heat to medium-low and bring to a simmer. Once the béchamel simmers and thickens, remove from the heat and season with salt and pepper.

3 Preheat oven to 390°F (200°C).

4 Put ⅛ of the Napa cabbage chunks on the bottom of each *cocotte*. Add, in turn, ⅛ of the canned salmon, ⅛ of the cheese, and ⅛ of the béchamel to each cocotte. Repeat to make layers. Sprinkle each with *panko* bread crumbs and bake in the oven until the top is nicely browned. Serve hot.

Baked Buttered Clams on the Half Shell

This is the basic finger food I make when having a stand-up party at my house. There is no need for a plate or fork, so guests can easily mingle and enjoy conversation with chilled white wine. When purchasing clams, check with your fishmonger if they have been cleaned of sand. If not, you can do this yourself at home. This is important, as the unpleasant grittiness of the sand ruins the dish.

SERVES FOUR

16 large clams, such as top neck clams (you may need more in case some do not open)

¼ cup white wine

About 4 Tbsp (2 oz./60 g) butter, softened

2 cloves garlic, minced

1 Tbsp chopped fresh parsley

Salt (optional)

2 Tbsp *panko* bread crumbs

2 thin slices lemon, each cut into 8 pieces

A good accompaniment to our meals is always wine, which my husband chooses depending on the taste of my dishes. We love to drink wine with Japanese cuisine too.

1 Scrub the clams in cold running water, drain and blot dry. If they have not been cleaned of sand, place them in salted water (made by combining 1 qt./1 L cold water and 2 Tbsp salt), cover and allow to stand in a dark, cool place for 1 hour for the sand and grit to be expelled. Drain the clams and set aside.

2 Cream together the butter, garlic and parsley. If using unsalted butter, add a pinch of salt. Keep in a cool place, but do not refrigerate.

3 Preheat oven to 390 to 425°F (200 to 220°C).

4 Put the clams in a medium saucepan over high heat and sprinkle with the white wine. Cover, and steam until the clams open. (Discard clams that do not open.) Remove the flesh from the shell. Separate each shell, and lay 16 half shells on a baking tray. Place a clam on each shell, top with equal portions of the butter mixture, and top with the *panko* bread crumbs. Bake until the bread crumbs are browned. If not brown after 5 minutes in the oven, broil them until the top is seared. Garnish each with a piece of lemon.

Oven-baked Potatoes and Sardines

In the freezer, I always keep a supply of tomato sauce, which I make in large batches. When I say "tomato sauce," I mean a concentrate in which only the flesh of canned tomatoes is mashed and simmered. It is useful when you want something "tomatoey." So here is a tomatoey, quickly-made appetizer. I'm not going to say this dish is Sicilian style, but it's good enough with a glass of Italian wine.

SERVES FOUR TO SIX

3 small to medium russet potatoes (about 1 ⅛ lbs./500 g)

5 oz. (140 g) canned sardines in oil

1 Italian tomato

½ cup Quick Tomato Sauce (page 98)

6 oz. (170 g) mozzarella, or any other cheese good for baking

Salt and black pepper

Butter for greasing

¼ cup *panko* bread crumbs

4 to 6 fresh basil leaves

1 Preheat oven to 390 °F (200 °C).

2 Scrub the potatoes in water. Wrap the unpeeled potatoes in food-safe plastic wrap and heat in a microwave for 13 minutes. Alternatively, boil or steam the unpeeled potatoes until soft. Cut them into thin rounds, about 2 slices for each serving.

3 Bring plenty of water to a boil in a medium saucepan. Have a medium bowl of ice water ready at the side. Score a shallow cross on the bottom of the tomato, drop into boiling water for a few seconds and immediately plunge into the ice water, using a slotted spoon or tongs. The tomato skin should peel off easily from the bottom. If not, plunge again into hot water, then ice water. Cut the tomato into 6 thin rounds, and each slice in half.

4 Cut the cheese into 4 to 6 slices (1 for each serving). If the cheese is shredded, divide equally into 4 to 6 portions.

5 Grease individual oven-proof dishes (or one large baking dish) with butter. Layer on each dish the potato rounds, fresh tomato slices, half the tomato sauce, sardines, cheese, and the remaining half of the tomato sauce. Sprinkle the top with *panko* bread crumbs. Bake in the oven for 8 to 10 minutes until the top is lightly browned and the ingredients are heated through. Top each serving with a basil leaf.

Deep-fried Scallops and Broccoli

This is a very simple dish of chopped scallops and broccoli wrapped in *nori* seaweed and fried. It's better not to put too many ingredients in the rolls. If they are too fat, they will fall apart when cut. One more thing—the batter should be put on just the ends of each roll, to retain the nori's shiny black color. Nori seaweed sheets have a pleasant nutty, briny flavor when heated. If you have them in your pantry, you can roll up any favorite food in them and deep-fry it as a snack.

MAKES EIGHT SMALL PIECES

2 oz. (60 g) scallops, thawed if frozen and chopped

½ broccoli

1 tsp salt

2 sheets dried *nori* seaweed (A regular nori sheet is 7 x 8 in./18.5 x 20.5 cm)

½ cup flour mixed with ½ cup water to make a paste

Oil for deep-frying

4 tsp *matcha* powdered green tea, mixed with 1 tsp salt

1 Bring plenty of water to a boil in a medium saucepan and add 1 tsp salt. Cut the broccoli into florets, blanch in the water and drain. Cut each floret into 4 to 5 pieces.

2 Preheat the oil for deep-frying to 340°F (170°C) in a heavy pot.

3 Cut each *nori* sheet in half. Trim a strip of about 1 in. (2 cm) from the short end of each half. Put the strip in the center of each half. (The strip makes the nori easier to roll.) Put about one broccoli floret and ¼ of the chopped scallops in the center of each half-sheet on top of the trimmed strip, then roll the nori sheet. Seal the edge with batter and dip both ends of the roll into the batter, leaving the center of the nori roll bare.

4 Deep-fry the rolls in oil until crisp. Drain on a rack and cut into halves. Arrange on a serving plate cut-side up, and serve the *matcha*-salt on the side.

Extra Crispy, Whisky-battered Seafood

Deep-fried foods are great for serving to guests. You can prepare the ingredients in advance and only need to mix the batter and deep-fry the morsels when the guests arrive. This batter contains whisky for an extra-crispy coating, contrasting with the extra-juicy seafood. The crispiness comes from the alcohol quickly evaporating in the hot oil, but you can reduce or eliminate the whisky and add water instead if you want to avoid alcohol.

8 shrimp, thawed if frozen
4 large scallops, thawed if frozen
1 bunch curly parsley

Oil for deep-frying
2 limes, cut in half
Salt to taste

Batter

¾ cup (100 g) flour
1 egg
Scant ½ cup whisky

1 Preheat the oil for deep-frying to 340 °F (170 °C) in a heavy pot.

2 If the shrimp is in the shell, peel off the shell except from the tail and cut off the tip of each tail using scissors. Remove the vein from each shrimp. Make several, shallow scores on the belly side and straighten out the shrimp to prevent them from curling up during frying. Cut each scallop around the edge and into rounds half as thick as the original scallop. Blot dry excess water from the shrimp and scallops. Cut fronds of parsley from the thicker stalks, rinse the fronds in water and blot dry.

3 Put the flour in a medium bowl and crack the egg into the bowl. Add the whisky and beat.

4 Dip the shrimp in the batter, deep-fry until crisp, and drain on a rack. Batter and deep-fry the scallops as well. Decrease the heat a bit to lower the oil temperature; batter the parsley, deep-fry until the batter is crisp, and drain on a rack.

5 Serve with lime halves and salt.

Mung Bean Noodles and Meat Balls in Soup

This is definitely my husband's favorite—a hearty, comforting soup that tastes as though it has simmered for a long time, though in fact it is only simmered for ten minutes or so. You can skip deep-frying the meat balls and cook them directly in the soup, but I recommend frying them since the texture becomes softer and they absorb the soup better. If you don't want to eat cooked lettuce, use watercress instead.

SERVES FOUR TO SIX

2 oz. (55 g) dried mung bean noodles
   (*harusame* in Japanese)

½ head iceberg lettuce

5 ½ oz. (150 g) bamboo shoots (try to find
   whole bamboo shoots packed in water)

4 large fresh shiitake mushrooms

1 *naganegi* onion (white part), or
   ½ other sweet onion

1 large knob ginger

½ cup potato starch (or cornstarch) for
   dusting

Oil for deep-frying

Soy sauce for seasoning

Meat balls

3 ½ oz. (100 g) ground beef

3 ½ oz. (100 g) ground pork

1 large knob ginger, minced

⅓ tsp salt

Black pepper to taste

Soup

2 bouillon cubes

1⅔ qts. (1.6 L) water

1 to 2 tsp soy sauce

1 Cut the mung bean noodles into 6-in. (15-cm) lengths with scissors. Tear the lettuce leaves into large pieces. Cut the bamboo shoots into thin slices. Remove the stem from mushrooms and cut into four pieces. Cut the onion into bite-size lengths. Mince the ginger.

2 Preheat the oil for deep-frying to 340°F (170°C).

3 Have ready the potato starch in a medium bowl. Combine the beef and pork in a large bowl and add the minced ginger, salt, and pepper. Stir well by hand until the mixture is blended. Scoop out about 2 Tbsp of the mixture and make a ball. Repeat for the rest. Dust the balls with potato starch, and deep-fry in the oil until the surface is slightly browned and crisp, and transfer onto a rack.

4 Bring 1⅔ qts. (1.6 L) water in a large pot to a boil, and dissolve the soup cubes. Add the bamboo shoots, mushrooms, onion, ginger, and noodles. Simmer gently for 10 to 15 minutes. Check the taste of the soup and add the soy sauce if needed. Add the lettuce leaves, bring to a boil once, and immediately turn off the heat. Eat while hot.

Seared Beef with Spicy Vegetables

We Japanese love *tataki* beef, which is beef seared, chilled in ice water, and sliced. It is enjoyed like sashimi with salad, by picking up a small bunch of crispy vegetables and herbs with the beef using chopsticks, and dipping it all in a soy-sauce-based dressing. I serve tataki beef already rolled around vegetables to make it easier to eat.

SERVES FOUR

1⅓ lbs. (600 g) beef striploin or rib-eye
1 Tbsp seasoning salt (or 1½ tsp regular salt)
½ head lettuce
1 pack radish sprouts, roots cut off
3 scallions, cut into thin slices
½ daikon radish, peeled, grated, and drained using a sieve
2 cloves garlic, peeled and chopped

Ponzu and Ginger Sauce
½ cup ponzu sauce
1 to 2 Tbsp grated ginger

1 Rub the seasoning salt all over the beef, let stand for 10 minutes and blot dry. Choose a large heavy pot and heat over high heat until smoking hot. Add the beef and sear all over. Plunge in ice water to chill thoroughly, remove and pat dry.

2 Crisp the lettuce in ice water, cut into thin slices and spread on a serving platter. Thinly slice the beef. Roll some of the radish sprouts, scallions, daikon radish and garlic in each beef slice and arrange on the bed of lettuce. Pour over the *ponzu* and ginger sauce.

Spicy Beef Rolls

Because I was raised in Kobe, a place renowned for producing great *wagyu* (Japanese beef), I've always been fond of dishes based around beef. Thinly sliced beef is not commonly sold at supermarkets in the West, but you can ask your butcher to slice it very thinly for you. My suggestion for which vegetables to use is not set in stone—use small spears of asparagus, shredded celery, or thinly sliced shiitake mushrooms. Find your favorite combination!

SERVES FOUR

14 oz. (400 g) round beef, sliced very thin

7 oz. (100 g) *enoki* mushrooms (or mung bean sprouts)

One 2-in. (5-cm) piece of carrot

4 scallions (or ½ bunch chives)

Salt and black pepper to taste

½ cup potato starch (or cornstarch) for dusting the rolls

2 tsp roasted sesame oil

Cilantro for garnishing

Spicy Sauce

1 tsp *dou ban jiang* (Chinese hot bean paste)

3 Tbsp sweet Chinese bean paste (*tian mian jiang*)

3 Tbsp chicken broth

1 Cut off the base of the *enoki* mushrooms, separating them. If using mung bean sprouts, remove the thin roots by hand, rinse in water and drain. Peel the piece of carrot, cut into thin slices, then cut the slices into thin matchsticks. Cut the scallion into 2-in. (5-cm) pieces.

2 Mix the spicy bean paste, sweet bean paste, and chicken broth together in a small bowl.

3 Spread out the beef slices on a cutting board and season them with salt and pepper. On each slice, place some carrot, enoki mushrooms, and scallions and roll up in the beef slice. Dust the rolls lightly with potato starch.

4 Heat a frying pan with the sesame oil and fry the beef rolls, starting seam-side down. Turn them until lightly browned all over. Add the spicy sauce to the pan, turning the beef rolls to coat them well. Arrange each roll on a serving plate and garnish with chopped cilantro.

I DON'T LIKE FUSS

My husband and I have to host a lot of people, and I love to cook for guests. Now that he's the prime minister, people say that they get a bit nervous when entering our house, so we always welcome our guests in jeans and casual shirts, with big, friendly smiles. I want my guests to enjoy good conversation and food, without having to worry about strict etiquette and manners. I always try to be myself, even at parties.

My party dishes are also very casual. I don't usually make recipes that have many layers of preparation but, rather, recipes that are an extension of the food I make every day. For example, I might take a dish that is popular with my family, then add a little twist by decorating it with a sprig of a tree from the garden, or perhaps serving it on a nicer antique plate, or using better ingredients than those we buy for ourselves.

When a guest says (in a very Japanese way) that they're sorry I'm working so hard in the kitchen, I am happy to assure them otherwise. I love to explain the secrets of quick and easy recipes, how much I enjoy cooking for guests, and how it is anything but a chore! On top of that, I am not the typical Japanese housewife, so instead of pretending to hesitate serving my food, I serve my dishes confidently, saying, "This is VERY good. You must try it!"

When my husband and I lived in the U.S., we met many men who praised their wives' cooking, which I thought was very sweet. I think my husband, too, is proud of my cooking. He may say that a certain dish is my best recipe, and that makes me happy. I remember once a guest asked him how I had made a dish, expecting that a lot of time and effort had gone into it. My husband immediately replied, "Oh, this is not particularly difficult to make, you just…" as if he had made it himself!

MY BEST RECIPES

I believe that for me, as for everyone, the best recipes are based on your life experiences. Learning cooking from American housewives, traveling to various countries and encountering great cuisine, I bring all these experiences together at our family table. These are my personal favorites.

Spareribs in Marmalade and Soy Sauce

Barbecued spareribs are great, but if you are looking for a variation, try this. The best thing about this recipe is that you only use a single pot and there's no grill to clean. Furthermore, you can make it in advance and reheat just before eating. Many Japanese don't like sweetness in meat dishes, but this one has just the right level of sweetness and zesty flavor.

SERVES FOUR

About 2 lbs. (900 g) pork spareribs, cut into pieces between the bones

3 cups water

1 bouillon cube

1 cup white wine

½ cup orange marmalade

5 Tbsp soy sauce

1 bunch watercress, cut into chunks

1 orange, thinly sliced

1   Place plenty of water in a large pot and bring to a boil. Put the spareribs in the water and cook for a minute. Drain and blot dry with paper towels.

2   Put the blanched spareribs in a heavy, thick-bottomed saucepan with the water, bouillon cube, and white wine. Turn the heat to high. Once the liquid simmers, skim off any foam from the surface and add the marmalade and soy sauce. Cover with a lid, that fits inside the pan, directly on the spareribs and simmer on high heat for 20 to 30 minutes, until the liquid in the pot is reduced to a thick glaze. As the liquid decreases, shake the pot vigorously from time to time to flip the spareribs and coat them evenly.

3   Serve on a platter and garnish with watercress and orange slices.

Chicken *alla Cacciatora*

This is my favorite dish. It can be cooked in advance and served when the guests are sitting at the table, so I can entertain without being stuck in my kitchen with no conversation. I use canned tomatoes and any vegetables that catch my eye in the market, or just whatever I have in the refrigerator!

SERVES FOUR

1⅓ lbs. (600 g) chicken thighs, bone-in (skin-on or skinless)

Seasoning salt (or salt and black pepper) to taste

1 pack button or cremini mushrooms, about 8 oz. (230 g)

2 zucchini

4 Japanese or Italian eggplants (or 1 to 2 American eggplants)

2 cloves garlic

2 to 3 small, red chili peppers, medium-hot

Two 14-oz. (400 g) canned whole or pureed tomatoes

⅓ cup red wine

10 large basil leaves

3 Tbsp olive oil

Salt

Curly parsley, for garnish

1   Cut the chicken into chunks and generously sprinkle with the seasoning salt. Trim the ends off the mushrooms. Cut the zucchini and eggplants into ½-in. (1.5-cm) rounds. Peel and press the garlic cloves with the flat part of the knife. Cut the chili peppers lengthwise and remove the seeds.

2   Put the olive oil, garlic and chili peppers in a large heavy pot over medium heat, cook until fragrant, and remove the garlic and chili peppers. Increase the heat to high, add the chicken chunks, and cook to nicely brown the surface all over. Add the mushrooms, zucchini, and eggplants and cook for a minute. Pour in the canned tomatoes, mashing them by hand if using whole tomatoes, and cook for a minute, stirring from time to time. Add the red wine and basil leaves and cook over medium heat for 40 minutes.

3   Serve in individual soup bowls and garnish with the curly parsley.

Breaded Lamb Chops

These fried lamb chops are breaded with *panko* bread crumbs mixed with dried oregano. I use seasoning salt, since it boosts the "lamby" flavor, but of course you can use regular salt and pepper. This is a very simple dish, though a key point is to tenderize the lamb with a mallet or the back of a heavy knife.

SERVES FOUR

10 frenched lamb chops

Seasoning salt (or salt and black pepper)

6 to 8 spears asparagus

2 tsp salt

Oil for deep-frying

1 onion, cut into rounds

4 sprigs Italian parsley

Breading

1 cup flour

2 eggs

1½ to 2 cups *panko* bread crumbs

1 to 1½ Tbsp dried oregano

1 Season the lamb chops with seasoning salt.

2 Put plenty of water in a large pot and bring to a boil, adding 2 tsp salt. Cut the hard base off the asparagus stalk and boil the spears until tender, but still crunchy. Drain and set aside.

3 Start heating the oil for deep-frying in a heavy pot to 340 °F (170 °C).

4 Put the flour in a medium bowl (or a small shallow tray). Beat the eggs in a separate medium bowl. Combine the *panko* bread crumbs and dried oregano in a third medium bowl.

5 Lightly pat dry the lamb chops with paper towels. Roll each chop in flour, eggs, and the panko-oregano mixture, and place on a tray or a dish. Coat each onion round in the same manner. Deep-fry the lamb chops and onion rounds in small batches until golden-brown and drain on a wire rack. Serve with the asparagus and Italian parsley.

Roasted Ham and Pineapple

This is a quick version of the classic American dish that I learned at a party in San Francisco years ago, and I am still making today. The fragrance of the whole cloves and the sweet pineapple deepens the ham's flavor as it is roasted and the juices combine. This recipe uses cured ham, but if you can find cured pork loin, try it for a leaner, meatier dish. I love to cut the leftovers in thin slices for sandwiches. The leftovers are also quite good as a topping for *ramen* noodles or fried rice!

SERVES FOUR OR FIVE

One 1½ lbs. (680 g) boneless ham (or cured loin), with
   skin removed if desired
Large handful whole cloves
11 oz. (310 g) canned pineapple, cut into small pieces
¾ cup syrup from the canned pineapple
⅓ cup sugar

1 Preheat oven to 325°F (180°C).

2 Score ⅛-in. (3-mm) deep crosshatch cuts on the top half of the roast and both ends. Lay in a baking dish and insert the cloves where the scores intersect. Cover the top with the pineapple pieces then the sugar, and pour over the syrup.

3 Transfer the dish to the oven. Roast for 30 minutes, then increase the oven temperature to 220°F (428°C) and roast for 10 minutes, basting occasionally. You may want some browned parts on the pineapple pieces, but if they brown too quickly, cover with foil. Remove the ham from the oven and allow to rest.

4 Remove all the cloves from the ham, cut it into thin slices and serve with pineapple pieces and syrup. When storing leftovers, keep in the syrup and refrigerate.

Scallop Steak with Garlic and Soy Sauce

I don't know if I could say this is a specialty, since it's so easy to make! I believe the best thing about scallops is the contrast between the texture of the crisp outside and the juicy inside, so just sauté briefly and be sure not to overcook. Serve them with a sweet, nutty mash of *kabocha* pumpkin and blanched broccoli.

SERVES FOUR

10 fresh scallops, thawed if frozen
Salt and black pepper
Flour for dusting
1 clove garlic, minced
2 Tbsp olive oil
Soy sauce

Mashed *kabocha* pumpkin
7 oz. (200 g) kabocha pumpkin
2 Tbsp butter

½ head broccoli, as garnish
1 tsp salt
½ bunch chives, as garnish

1 Cut the *kabocha* pumpkin into large chunks. (If it is too hard to cut, heat in a microwave for 30 seconds to make cutting easy.) Peel, and heat in a microwave for about 5 minutes until tender. Mash and stir in the butter. Keep warm.

2 Put plenty of water in a medium pot, bring to a boil, and add 1 tsp salt. Cook the broccoli until tender, but still crunchy. Drain and set aside.

3 Cut the scallops crosswise in half. Season with salt and pepper, dust with flour and remove excess flour by patting.

4 Put the garlic and olive oil in a large frying pan and heat over medium-high heat. When the oil is hot, add the scallop halves and sauté both sides until golden brown. Sprinkle with the soy sauce, shake the pan and remove from the heat.

5 Serve the scallops on individual serving plates and top with the chives. Arrange the broccoli and the mashed kabocha pumpkin on the side.

Pork Tenderloin Poached in Black Tea with Balsamic Vinegar

I hesitate to say this again, but this is a great party dish made so easily. The sauce contains balsamic vinegar, sugar, and soy sauce, and adds a complex flavor to the pork. I love to combine balsamic vinegar and soy sauce, and I use the combination even for classic Japanese dishes. Balsamic vinegar varies in sweetness depending on its age, so adjust to taste with the sugar.

SERVES FOUR

1 lb. (about 500 g) pork tenderloin
About 3 bags black tea, any kind
8 cups water
⅓ cup balsamic vinegar
⅓ cup soy sauce
2 Tbsp or more sugar
½ bunch watercress
4 tsp grated wasabi

Japanese antique porcelain is great for serving Western-style food, too. The blue and white color combination beautifully enhances the food's appearance.

1 Pour 8 cups of boiling water into a pot and add the teabags. Brew a rather strong tea, then remove the teabags. Add the pork tenderloin to the pot and turn heat to high. Bring the liquid to a boil and cook the tenderloin for 10 minutes. Turn off the heat and leave the tenderloin to cool in the tea.

2 In a bowl, mix together the balsamic vinegar, soy sauce, and sugar until combined.

3 Take the tenderloin out of the pot and blot dry. Slice thinly against the grain and arrange on a serving plate. Garnish with watercress and a dab of wasabi, and pour the balsamic vinegar sauce over the top.

King Crab and Mushrooms in Cream

Many Japanese, including me, look forward to the crab season. In Japanese, king crab is called "taraba," which means "cod place," since the king crab is often caught where cod is fished. This dish looks gorgeous, but to let you in on a secret, I just simmer it in white wine and add cream. The saltiness comes naturally from the crab.

SERVES FOUR

2 ¼ lbs. (1 kg) legs and body of king crab
7 oz. (200 g) button mushrooms
2 cups white wine
1 cup heavy cream
2 Tbsp vegetable oil
½ cup chopped scallions

1 Chop the crab legs into 2½-in. (6-cm) lengths. Chop the body into chunks. Trim the hard base of the mushrooms and cut in half vertically.

2 Pour the vegetable oil in a large pot over medium-high heat and swirl to coat the bottom. Add the crab and cook for 1 to 2 minutes. Add the mushrooms and cook for another 1 to 2 minutes. Pour over the wine, and when the amount of wine has been reduced by half, add the heavy cream and bring to a boil. Tun off the heat and stir in the chopped scallions.

I began making ceramics while living in the U.S. There was
a kiln near my place that I often visited, and imitated what
the artists were doing. I love to work with stained glass, too.
Once you get the basics, you can go your own way and create
what you want, sort of like cooking!

Curry Pilaf with Short-grain Rice

This pilaf is cooked in an electric cooker, so you don't need to watch over it while it is cooking, making this an ideal party dish. Pilaf made with short-grain rice (which may be labeled as sushi rice in food stores) is fluffy, but has more moisture than a pilaf cooked with long-grain rice. The sautéed banana, added at the last minute, gives the dish an extra kick.

SERVES FOUR TO SIX

3 cups short-grain rice	1 to 2 Tbsp curry powder
13 oz. (360 g) trimmed pork belly or shoulder	2 tsp soy sauce
1 onion	2 bananas
1 clove garlic	2 Tbsp almond slices, toasted
3 cups chicken broth	2 Tbsp dried raisins
1½ Tbsp vegetable oil	½ bunch cilantro, chopped

1 Rinse the short-grain rice in several changes of cold water and drain using a sieve. Leave for an hour.

2 Cut the pork into small cubes. Mince the onion and garlic.

3 Heat 1 Tbsp vegetable oil in a large frying pan over medium heat and add the onion, garlic, and pork. Sprinkle in the curry powder and soy sauce, and mix well.

4 Place the contents of the pan into an electric rice cooker (leave the pan unwashed), add the rice and chicken broth, and cook using the regular cooking mode.

5 Cut the banana into small pieces. Put ½ Tbsp oil in the same frying pan and quickly fry the banana. When the rice is cooked, place the banana on top in the rice cooker and mix from the bottom using a cutting motion. Do not stir the rice or it will become sticky.

6 Serve on a platter with toasted almond slices, raisins, and chopped cilantro.

MOTTAINAI SPIRIT

ottainai is a Japanese word that means something like, "it's a shame it's being wasted when it's still useful." The concept is a kind of national spirit in Japan, and the word is pervasive in everyday conversation and very much part of the national identity. I try to apply the mottainai spirit to my daily life, and of course to my cooking. I've been using my kitchen knife for more than thirty years. After sharpening countless times, the blade has been reduced to about one third its original size, which makes it feel more comfortable in my hand. I once bought a new knife, but eventually went back to using my old one. My three cast iron frying pans and aluminum steamer were purchased in the U.S., and they have also been with me more than thirty years. The pickling jars I use were originally instant coffee containers handed down by my mother. I can't throw these things away.

When someone sends me a gift, I think of what I can do with the box. Some people may hesitate to admit something like that, but not me. I love to make the most of things, and I do so also for my cooking. I start by looking at the leftovers and scraps in the drawer of the refrigerator, and wait for a flash of inspiration for the day's meal.

I also stock a lot of sauces in my refrigerator. I try not to run out of our family's favorite dressing (Hatoyama Dressing on page 98) and basic *dashi* stock (dashi is like chicken stock in the West). I usually shop once a week, and that's the day that I really have to work. That day I blanch most of the vegetables I buy in salted water, then cut them into certain lengths. They go immediately into containers in the refrigerator, or are tossed with salt and roasted sesame oil to make Korean *namul*. In this way, I don't need to see wilted or shriveled vegetables in my refrigerator. It is said that potatoes should not be frozen, since the thawed texture becomes spongy. However, if you slice them very thinly, this doesn't happen. Lay plastic wrap on a sheet tray, make very thin slices using a slicer, and lay the slices on the tray overlapping each other. Wrap tightly and freeze. You can then cook them in a frying pan whenever you want.

Thus my quick and easy dishes are made by rational and economic work, based on the mottainai spirit. Of course, if you cook three meals every day and can buy and use up fresh ingredients, that is best. But these days, unless you aspire to creating a top restaurant at home, applying the mottainai spirit helps make good, delicious meals quickly, easily, and economically.

OUR COMFORT FOOD

My parents raised me on bread more than rice, and I didn't eat a lot of standard Japanese dishes while I was growing up. I started making them when I was living in the U.S. and found myself craving Japanese food, but I adapted them to my own tastes and what I had available in San Francisco. Now those recipes have become our family comfort foods.

Vegetables Pickled in Vinegar, Soy Sauce, and *Dashi* Stock

When I open the vegetable drawer in my fridge and find a few vegetable leftovers, it's time to make pickles. A little wilted? They are still good enough for homemade pickles. These pickles contain *dashi* stock, so they are not meant to be stored for a long time. Pickling is the perfect way to ensure you don't waste any food.

About 2 ¼ lbs. (1 kg) vegetables
2 tsp salt

Pickling liquid

- 3 cups rice vinegar or white wine vinegar
- ½ cup sugar
- 1 cup *dashi* stock or water
- ¼ cup soy sauce
- ¼ cup white wine
- 1 tsp balsamic vinegar (optional)

Suggested vegetables

Carrot, onion, zucchini, cucumber, celery, cauliflower, bell pepper, radish, lotus root, *myoga* ginger buds

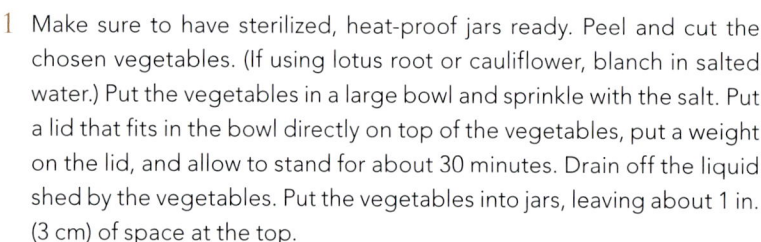

1 Make sure to have sterilized, heat-proof jars ready. Peel and cut the chosen vegetables. (If using lotus root or cauliflower, blanch in salted water.) Put the vegetables in a large bowl and sprinkle with the salt. Put a lid that fits in the bowl directly on top of the vegetables, put a weight on the lid, and allow to stand for about 30 minutes. Drain off the liquid shed by the vegetables. Put the vegetables into jars, leaving about 1 in. (3 cm) of space at the top.

2 Combine all ingredients of the pickling liquid in a pot and bring to a simmer. Pour the pickling liquid into sterilized jars to the very top, close the lids tight, and put aside until they are cool. Let the vegetables marinate in the refrigerator at least one whole day. Keep about 2 months in a cool place before opening.

Sautéed Vegetables in Sesame Oil

This is a dish especially for using leftover root vegetables from the fridge, instead of making pickles (page 78). You don't need to strictly follow the vegetable quantities below; just use what you have. Slice them thinly and sauté them over high heat. I love to use sesame oil for sautéing vegetables, and garnishing them with a generous sprinkling of ground, toasted sesame seeds. The toasted seeds add a savory, nutty flavor to the vegetables.

SERVES FOUR

A 12-in. (30-cm) piece of *gobo* burdock root
½ carrot
1 stick celery, with its leaves if any
1 joint lotus root, about 3 in. (7.5 cm) long
1 pack radish sprouts (optional)
2 Tbsp roasted sesame oil
2 Tbsp sugar
3 ½ Tbsp soy sauce
1 Tbsp white sesame seeds, toasted and ground

Other suggested vegetables

Bell pepper, parsnip, asparagus, zucchini, celery, or any dense, crunchy vegetable. If you would like to add cooking greens such as spinach, bok choy, or chard, first blanch them in salted water, then add them to the pan at the last minute of sautéing.

1 Peel the carrot and burdock root. Separate the celery leaves and cut into chunks. Remove the tough strings from the celery stalk. Using a vegetable peeler, peel off thin strips of carrot, burdock root, and celery. Slice the lotus root into thin rounds. Trim off the ends of the radish sprouts.

2 In a large frying pan, heat the roasted sesame oil until the surface of the oil becomes rippled. Add the carrot, burdock root, celery, and lotus root and cook until tender, but still a little crunchy. Add the sugar, soy sauce, and radish sprouts, and swirl the pan a few times. Sprinkle generously with ground toasted sesame seeds.

Cod, Tofu, and Shiitake Mushrooms Steamed in *Kombu*

Hokkaido, Japan's northern island and my husband's original constituency, is famous for an abundance of fresh seafood—and for producing *kombu* kelp. It is essential for making *dashi* stock (page 98), but once in a while I enjoy kombu in this way, using it as a plate and a seasoning at the same time. Cod and tofu especially absorb the wonderful flavor of the kombu, and blend perfectly to make a classic Japanese combination.

MAKES TWO *KOMBU* PLATES

8 oz. (230 g) cod fillets, bones removed

½ block soft tofu, about 6 oz. (170 g)

4 large fresh shiitake mushrooms

3 ½ oz. (100 g) *maitake* mushrooms

1 bunch fresh spinach

2 tsp salt

6 to 8 ginkgo nuts (optional)

2 large pieces *kombu* kelp, each about 12 in. (30 cm) long

2 Tbsp sake

Ponzu sauce (store-bought) to taste

The wooden barrels left over after making miso are great for chilling sake with plenty of ice. With some bamboo leaves cut from the garden, my table becomes fancy without any hassle.

1   Soak the *kombu* kelp in cold water to soften for about 30 minutes. Tie each end with kitchen twine to make a boat-shaped dish.

2   Cut the cod and tofu into 4 pieces. Trim off the tough stem of the shiitake mushrooms and cut each in half lengthwise. Separate the *maitake* mushrooms into chunks. Put plenty of water in a large pot, bring to a boil, and add 2 tsp salt. Blanch the spinach, drain, and dip in ice water. Lightly squeeze the spinach by hand and cut into chunks.

3   Have a large steamer ready. Arrange the cod, tofu, shiitake mushrooms, maitake mushrooms and ginkgo nuts (if using) in the kombu dishes. Sprinkle with the sake. Place in the steamer, cover, and cook for 10 to 15 minutes, adding the spinach at the last minute. Serve and eat by dipping the cod, tofu, and vegetables in the *ponzu* sauce.

Rice Bowl with Soy-marinated Tuna

If you haven't tasted soy-marinated tuna, you're missing out. It's more akin to meat than fish. You don't need sashimi-quality tuna, and it is acceptable even if the bright red color darkens a little through oxidizing. I always make this with some leftovers from *maguro* sashimi or carpaccio. Many substitutions can be made, such as grated ginger instead of grated wasabi, or tahini paste instead of ground sesame seeds. If you can't find *shiso* leaves and *nori* seaweed, chopped scallions work well as a substitute.

SERVES FOUR

14 oz. (400 g) fillet of fresh tuna, cut into slices

Marinade
  2 Tbsp white sesame seeds, toasted and ground
  3 to 4 Tbsp soy sauce
  4 tsp grated wasabi

4 to 6 *shiso* leaves
2 sheets dried *nori* seaweed (A regular nori sheet is
    7 x 8 in./18.5 x 20.5 cm)
4 bowls hot cooked rice

1 Combine all ingredients of the marinade and marinate the tuna slices for 10 to 15 minutes.

2 Cut the *shiso* leaves into ribbons. Cut the *nori* seaweed (toasting the sheets lightly over a flame makes the nori more flavorful) into thin sticks.

3 On top of each bowl of cooked rice, scatter the nori sticks. Arrange the marinated tuna slices on top and garnish with the shiso.

Maguro Burgers

M*aguro* burgers don't require expensive tuna; any lean part of the tuna, frozen or leftover, works well. Many fishermen use a combination of local fish for this kind of recipe, cooking and eating them in the boat after their catch. I use leftover tuna for an upscale version, but salmon or any rich, meaty fish is a good substitute.

MAKES 4 BURGERS

10 ½ oz. (300 g) tuna
½ cup chopped scallions
1 small knob ginger, grated
1 clove garlic, grated
2 Tbsp miso
1 tsp salad oil for frying
2 tsp grated wasabi
Soy sauce

1 With a knife, chop the tuna into small pieces. Mix the scallions, ginger, garlic, and miso with the chopped tuna and form into 4 patties.

2 Heat oil in a frying pan and fry the tuna patties on both sides until well-browned. Serve with the grated wasabi and soy sauce.

Korean *Gyoza* Dumplings

Gyoza are pan-fried Chinese dumplings—with some adaptation to Japanese taste—that all Japanese adore. People from the Korean Peninsula have their own version of gyoza, called *mandu*, which I found at a Korean restaurant near our house. I liked them so much, I tried to recreate them at home. The result was great—fluffy and succulent inside, with a crispy, browned wrapper. The Japanese-style Chinese dumplings with a Korean twist really hit the spot for all of us and are a regular at our table.

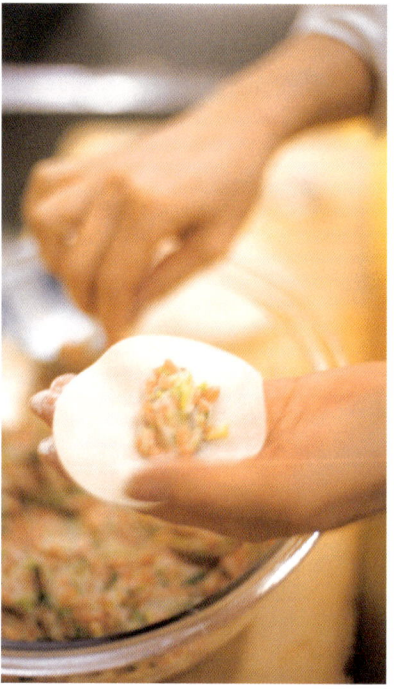

SERVES FOUR

24 dumpling wrappers, thawed if frozen
Flour for dusting

Filling

3 oz. (85 g) chopped kimchi (or 2 large leaves fresh Napa cabbage)
5½ oz. (150 g) ground pork
1 clove garlic, grated
1½ oz. (50 g) grated *yamaimo* mountain potato (or mashed tofu)
½ cup minced scallions

Dipping Sauce

3 Tbsp soy sauce
1½ Tbsp rice vinegar
½ tsp sugar
1 tsp *dou ban jiang* (Chinese hot bean paste) or ¼ tsp Korean chili powder
1 tsp roasted sesame oil
1 clove garlic, grated

Vegetable oil for frying

1 If using the fresh Napa cabbage leaves instead of chopped kimchi, blanch them in salted boiling water (1 tsp salt per 2 qts./2 L water), drain, squeeze, and cut into small pieces.

2 Combine the kimchi (or Napa cabbage), ground pork, garlic, scallions, and *yamaimo* mountain potato in a large bowl and stir by hand until the mixture becomes somewhat sticky.

3 Spoon 1 to 2 tsp of the filling in the center of each wrap, damp the edges, fold, and seal by pinching the edges into frills. Lay on a dish and dust with flour so that they do not stick together.

4 Heat a large frying pan, and coat with 1 tsp vegetable oil over high heat. Lay the dumplings (only the amount that fits into the pan in a single layer) and fry for 1 to 2 minutes, until the bottom of the dumplings is slightly dried and a bit browned. Pour in ½ cup water between the dumplings, cover with a lid, and fry for 6 to 8 minutes until the water is almost evaporated. Uncover, and sprinkle with a little vegetable oil and sear the bottom of the dumplings until brown. Serve with the dipping sauce.

Nikujaga Beef and Potatoes, Hatoyama-style

You may already know this Japanese classic. It's easy to make, made of relatively cheap, accessible ingredients, and wonderfully appetizing. My own recipe may contain some ingredients hard to find outside Japan, so feel free to omit them, since *nikujaga* should be simple. For the beef, I always use scraps, the very thin cuts of meat sold in the meat corner at supermarkets in Japan. Leftover steak cut into cubes also works well. I love simmering the ingredients until the onion is meltingly soft and serving them on hot rice to make a meat-and-potato rice bowl.

SERVES FOUR

7 oz. (200 g) thinly sliced beef (any cut is fine)
3 small russet potatoes, peeled and cut into chunks
1 medium onion, cut into chunks

Optional

   4 oz. (110 g) *shirataki* (noodle-like white
      konnyaku, found in Asian markets)
   1 cup mushrooms, such as *shimeji, enoki,*
      or oyster mushrooms, cut into chunks
   ½ bunch *shungiku* greens

2 Tbsp sugar
2 Tbsp sake
3 Tbsp *mirin*
4 Tbsp soy sauce
3 ½ cups water

1   Soak the potatoes in cold water for 10 minutes and drain. Wrap the potatoes in food-safe plastic wrap and microwave on high for 4 minutes, or boil until a skewer pierces them easily.

2   If using *shirataki*, sprinkle with salt, rub well and rinse in cold water. Blanch in lightly salted boiling water for a few seconds. Drain and cut into roughly 4-in. (10-cm) lengths. Cut off any tough parts of the mushrooms and separate into chunks.

3   Pour 3½ cups water into a medium pot and put over high heat. Add the beef. When the water begins to boil, lower the heat to maintain a gentle simmer and skim any foam that rises to the surface. Add the sugar, sake, *mirin*, and soy sauce. Add the onion and shirataki (if using) and cook for 10 minutes. Add the potatoes and mushrooms (if using) and cook for 15 to 20 minutes. Add the *shungiku* greens (if using), cook for seconds and turn off the heat.

4   Arrange the meat and vegetables in a serving bowl and spoon some of the simmering liquid over the top.

Cooked Rice with Fish and *Kombu*

Rice cooked with seasonal vegetables, tofu, and/or fish may be the original Japanese comfort food. The white rice absorbs the natural juices of the ingredients as they are cooked together, becoming fragrant but not overly seasoned. In Japan we appreciate local, seasonal fish that is only found in one place at one time. My family adores *kin-kin* from the northern part of Japan. It has a pleasant richness to it that coats the rice beautifully. But kin-kin is hard to get, even for me in Japan so my best alternative in Tokyo, or in the West, is tilefish. Cod and salmon are also wonderful cooked with rice. The fish should be very fresh, without a strong fishy smell.

SERVES FOUR

3 cups short-grain rice

1 whole cleaned tilefish, or 4 fillets tilefish (about 1 lb./450 g), skin-on or skinless, bones removed

1 piece dried *kombu* kelp

Salt

4 *shiso* leaves

1   Rinse the rice with several changes of water, drain using a sieve and set aside for at least 20 minutes.

2   Meanwhile, generously sprinkle the fish with salt and leave for 20 minutes. Broil or grill on both sides. (If using a whole fish, make a broth from the leftover bones. Put 4 ¼ cups water and the large bones in a pot over medium heat and simmer for 5 minutes, strain, and let cool.)

3   In an electric rice cooker, add the rice and 4 cups water (or the fish broth from step 2). Add the *kombu* and fish and cook the rice on the regular setting. When the rice is cooked, leave it for 10 mintues to let it steam. Open the lid, remove the kombu, and lightly mix with a cutting motion (do not stir).

4   Serve in individual rice bowls and top with shredded *shiso* leaves.

Rice Bowl with Pork, Tofu, and *Edamame*

After enjoying a variety of dishes at a party or restaurant, the Japanese often want to finish with a bowl of hot rice. Since this is served at the end of a long meal, the portions are small. Here's my version of it, using Chinese sweet bean paste (*tian mian jiang*) and pork—and it's so good that everyone is going to ask for another helping! It is also ideal as a quick, convenient lunch.

MAKES 1 SMALL SERVING

1½ to 2 oz. (50 g) pork loin, cut into thin slices

⅛ block tofu, about 2 oz. (60 g)

1 scallion

2 Tbsp *dashi* stock or water

1 Tbsp *tian mian jiang* (Chinese sweet bean paste)

½ sheet dried *nori* seaweed (A regular nori sheet is 7 x 8 in./18.5 x 20.5 cm)

1 Tbsp cooked *edamame* beans

Small bowl of hot cooked rice

1 Bring a small pot of water to a boil. Put the pork in a sieve, put the sieve over a sink, and pour the boiling water over the pork to blanch it. Cut the tofu into 4 pieces. Cut the scallion into chunks.

2 In a small pot, combine the *dashi* stock or water with the Chinese sweet bean paste. Add the pork, tofu, and scallion, bring to a boil and immediately turn off the heat.

3 Tear the *nori* seaweed by hand and scatter on the bowl of cooked rice. Add the pork and tofu, and top with the *edamame* beans.

LOVE AND COOKING

I believe that our perspectives profoundly influence our lives. In cooking, if you feel making food is a hassle, it will surely become a hassle, and the food that you make with a negative mindset will not taste good. If you continue to make such food, you will dislike cooking more and more. In life, you often have to change your mindset to improve your circumstances. The same can be said for cooking.

I have had some difficult times as a result of being too stubborn and inflexible. I am a positive person, but I used to be too direct, insisting on my own opinion and forcing it on others. My husband and son had a hard time with me, but they were the ones who ultimately changed me. Perhaps they never said anything to me directly, but the time we spent eating together played an important role in patching up, maintaining, and renewing our family relationships. At the dinner table we shared a common love, influenced each other, and grew to be better people. I appreciate how lucky I have been to have had the chance to cook for my family and share so much important time together.

My husband has been an advocate of love his whole life. He has always lamented that there is increasingly less love in this world. However, these days, I think many people are coming to realize the true meaning of love and friendship. To understand others, or at least to try to, without denying them even if you don't agree with them, is an important human virtue. I think families are a good example of that virtue on a smaller, more personal scale. And in my family, without doubt, food plays an important role. I have cooked for years for my family, thinking of it as one way of expressing my love. We are bound together, more or less, over food.

Although I give all my love unconditionally to my family, in the end I realize that it is me who receives the most love from them, through their happy, joyful smiles, as they chat over their food at the dinner table. I can't stop thinking of how grateful I am to them all. They are the inspiration for all my recipes, and will be my motivation for cooking forever. And they are the ones who taught me what it means to love.

SUPPLEMENTAL RECIPES

Hatoyama Dressing

5 Tbsp red wine vinegar
1 cup safflower oil, or any other
   vegetable oil
3 Tbsp soy sauce
1 pack (0.7 oz./19 g) powdered Italian
   salad dressing mix

This recipe makes about 1½ cups of dressing. I just mix the ingredients into an empty red wine vinegar bottle, screw the cap shut, and shake to make the dressing. I use "Good Seasons" brand dressing mix, but if you don't use it, add powdered, or freshly grated, onion, garlic, celery, and salt into a bowl and adjust the amounts to taste. Adding herbs such as oregano or parsley is a good idea. You can make the dressing even tastier by using Tosa soy sauce instead of regular soy sauce. To make Tosa soy sauce, put one cup of soy sauce in a bowl and add one cup of bonito flakes and leave to steep overnight. The next day, strain out the bonito flakes and use 3 Tbsp of the Tosa soy sauce in place of regular soy sauce.

Quick Tomato Sauce

2 cans or more tomatoes, either whole
   or diced, but not seasoned with salt
   or herbs

First, strain the canned tomatoes using a sieve, pressing down a little to separate the fruit and juice. Transfer only the fruit to a saucepan and cook for about 20 minutes over medium heat, flattening the tomatoes with a wooden spatula. You may need to adjust the heat to avoid scorching the bottom. Remove from the heat and allow to cool to room temperature. I always divide the sauce into small batches and store in the freezer. It keeps for about 2 months. The leftover juice can be simmered with bacon, cabbage, onion, and bay leaves to make soup.

Dashi Stock

2½ oz. (70 g) dried *kombu* kelp
3½ oz. (100 g) dried bonito flakes
3 qts. (3 L) water

My *dashi* stock is twice as rich as ordinary dashi. I make it once or twice a week and store it in instant coffee jars in the refrigerator. First, pour 3 qts. (3 L) water into a large pot and soak the *kombu* in it overnight, or for at least 8 hours. The next day, put the pot with the kombu still in it over medium heat. Just before the water simmers, remove the kombu. When the water boils, add the dried bonito flakes. Bring back to a boil once, then turn off the heat. Leave undisturbed until the bonito flakes naturally sink to the bottom. Strain through a fine-mesh sieve lined with a doubled cheese-cloth or paper towel. After the stock has cooled you can store it in containers in the refrigerator.

GLOSSARY

alla cacciatora
Chicken seared and cooked with herbs, mushrooms, and wine with or without tomatoes. *Alla cacciatora* means "hunter-style" in Italian.

buri
Yellowtail fish, *Seriola quinqueradiata*, appreciated in Japan for its fatty, sweet taste and filling tuna-like meatiness. Eaten raw as sushi or sashimi, grilled as teriyaki, or simmered in a hotpot.

daikon radish
A giant variety of radish, very mild and sweet, easily found in gourmet and Asian supermarkets.

dashi stock
A pale broth used in Japanese cooking, see recipe on page 98.

dou ban jiang
A spicy Chinese paste made from red peppers, fava beans, rice, and soybeans, often labeled as "hot bean paste."

edamame beans
Young, green soy beans that come in the pod. Eaten after boiling in salted water, they are a favorite summer vegetable in Japan.

en cocotte
A cocotte is a small, French heatproof dish in which food is baked in individual portions.

enoki mushrooms
Noodle-thin mushrooms, edible raw.

gobo burdock root
A very long, thin brown root vegetable, also known as burdock.

gochujang
A Korean condiment made from fermented red peppers, sticky rice, and soybeans.

gyoza
Japanese pan-fried dumplings, originally a Chinese specialty that is now popular all over Japan.

harusame
Fine, transparent noodles made of mung beans, often sold as "bean threads."

Jjigae
Korean hotpot, flavored with kimchi, *gochujang*, or another Korean condiment.

kabocha pumpkin
A Japanese squash shaped like a pumpkin but with a thin, edible skin. Acorn squash or small pumpkins (they must be peeled first) can be used as a substitute.

kalguksu
Korean wheat-flour noodles. Japanese udon noodles can be used as a substitute.

kimchi
A Korean pickle of Napa cabbage in fermented chili pepper paste.

kombu kelp
A variety of giant kelp seaweed, very rich in *umami*, sold dried in Asian supermarkets. Umami is a fifth taste (in addition to salty, sweet, sour, and bitter), found in meats, seafood, cheeses, fermented bean products, tomatoes, seaweed, and some mushrooms.

maguro
Maguro is any red-fleshed tuna, and it's a good idea to use yellowfin tuna, also called *ahi*, rather than the overfished bluefin tuna.

maitake mushrooms
Flavorful mushrooms with layers of flaky, brown "leaves," also known as "hen-of-the-woods."

mirin
Sweet, syrupy rice wine brewed from sticky rice, almost never drunk on its own but used as a sweetener in cooking.

miso

A fermented soybean paste that comes in hundreds of varieties, I like to use *hatcho* miso, a very dark and dense miso made entirely from soybeans.

mitsuba herb

A celery-like herb related to parsley. Can be substituted with celery, parsley, or watercress.

naganegi onion

A long, thick variety of scallion that is much sweeter and milder than ordinary scallions. It is hard to find outside Japan, so use any sweet bulb onion, such as Vidalia, or even very thinly sliced red onion as a substitute.

nori seaweed

A crisp sheet of dried seaweed, used to roll sushi.

panko bread crumbs

Coarse, Japanese-style breadcrumbs that make a crispier coating than finer breadcrumbs. If you can't find them, you can make them by coarsely grating ordinary white bread.

ponzu sauce

A sauce made from soy sauce, citrus juice, and *dashi* stock.

potato starch

Pure starch extracted from potatoes. Makes a crispier coating for fried foods than flour or cornstarch.

sake

Japanese wine brewed from fermented rice. There are drier sakes and sweeter sakes, but any kind will do for most recipes.

seasoning salt

A blended salt mixture with various spice and herbs. Lawry's seasoning salt is used for the recipes in this book.

shabu-shabu

A kind of hotpot where meat or fish is briefly swished in hot broth (making a "shabu-shabu" sound) and dipped in a sauce before being eaten.

shimeji mushrooms

Thin mushrooms with a mild flavor. Ordinary white or brown mushrooms can be a substitute.

shirataki

A kind of noodle made from *konnyaku*, a Japanese root vegetable with a high fiber content and very few calories.

shiso leaves

An herb closely related to basil and mint, and with a flavor a little like both. If you can't find it, try to order seeds and add it to your herb garden. It grows very easily.

shungiku greens

Tender, edible greens from a variety of chrysanthemums. Can be substituted with spinach or Swiss chard. (Swiss chard may need to be cooked a little longer than shungiku.)

tian mian jiang

A dark-colored Chinese flavoring paste made from fermented wheat and soybeans, sold as "sweet bean sauce" or "duck sauce."

wagyu

Japanese beef, made from a special breed of cattle raised under carefully controlled conditions, with a mild flavor and very rich marbling. You can use U.S. prime grade beef as a substitute, though it's not as well marbled.

wasabi

A green root that grates into a surprisingly hot paste, available as a powder in many supermarkets, but fresh is best if you can find it.

yamaimo mountain potato

A kind of yam that is crisp and edible raw, a little like jicama, but more gelatinous and less sweet. It is also used grated as a binder and a topping.

C O N V E R S I O N S

LENGTH

Imperial	Metric
⅛ in.	3 mm
¼ in.	6 mm
½ in.	1 cm
1 in.	2.5 cm
1 ½ in.	4 cm
2 in.	5 cm
2 ½ in.	6 cm
3 in.	7.5 cm
4 in.	10 cm
5 in.	13 cm
6 in.	15 cm
8 in.	20 cm

OVEN TEMPERATURE

Fahrenheit (°F)	Celsius (°C)	Gas Mark
250	120	½
275	130	1
300	150	2
325	160	3
340	170	3
350	180	4
375	190	5
390	200	6
400	210	6
425	220	7
450	230	8
475	245	9

VOLUME

U.S.	Metric
⅛ teaspoon	0.5 ml
¼ teaspoon	1 ml
½ teaspoon	2.5 ml
¾ teaspoon	4 ml
1 teaspoon	5 ml
1 tablespoon (3 teaspoons)	15 ml
¼ cup (4 tablespoons)	60 ml
⅓ cup	80 ml
½ cup	120 ml
⅔ cup	160 ml
¾ cup	180 ml
1 cup	240 ml
1 ¼ cups	300 ml
1 ½ cups	360 ml
2 cups (1 pint)	480 ml
2 ½ cups	600 ml
3 cups	720 ml
4 cups (1 quart)	1,000 ml (1 liter)
1 gallon (4 quarts)	4 liters

WEIGHT

Ounces	Grams
¼	7
½	15
⅔	20
1	30
2	60
3	85
4	120
5	140
6	170
7	200
8	230
9	255
10	280
11	310
12	340
14	400
16 oz. (1 lb.)	450
2 lbs.	900
2 ¼ lbs.	1,000 g (1 kg)

INDEX

Bold type indicates an item that is defined in the glossary (pp. 99–100).

Hair-styling and makeup on the cover: Hiromi Itaya (ITAYA)
Contributing Editor: Noriko Yokota
Translations: Derek Wilcox
Copyediting: Matthew Cotterill and Lidia Rényi

PHOTO (PAGE 8): Kyodo News

本書は『ようこそ「鳩山レストラン」へ』(講談社)を元にして、
追加撮影・取材のうえ、再構成したものです。

(英文版) ようこそ「鳩山レストラン」へ
Home Cooking with Japan's First Lady

2010年2月25日　第 1 刷発行

著　者　　鳩山 幸
撮　影　　半田広徳
発行者　　廣田浩二
発行所　　講談社インターナショナル株式会社
　　　　　〒112–8652　東京都文京区音羽 1–17–14
　　　　　電話　03–3944–6493 (編集部)
　　　　　　　　03–3944–6492 (マーケティング部・業務部)
　　　　　ホームページ　www.kodansha-intl.com
印刷・製本所　　大日本印刷株式会社